AXIS PARENT GUIDES

A PARENT'S GUIDE TO INFLUENCERS

A PARENT'S GUIDE TO

INFLUENCERS

Tyndale House Publishers
Carol Stream, Illinois

Visit Tyndale online at tyndale.com.

Visit Axis online at axis.org.

Tyndale and Tyndale's quill logo are registered trademarks of Tyndale House Ministries.

A Parent's Guide to Influencers

For information about special discounts for bulk purchases, please contact Tyndale House Publishers at csresponse@tyndale.com, or call 1-855-277-9400.

Library of Congress Cataloging-in-Publication Data

A catalog record for this book is available from the Library of Congress.

ISBN 978-1-4964-6718-8

Printed in the United States of America

28	27	26	25	24	23	22
7	6	5	4	3	2	1

70% of teens think that YouTubers
are more reliable than celebrities
and 88% of consumers trust online
recommendations as much as face-to-
face recommendations. Social media
influencers are real people, and
they're more likely to be authentic
and to interact with their audience,
so brands are starting to take note.

DIGITAL INFORMATION WORLD

CONTENTS

A LETTER FROM AXIS

Dear Reader,

We're Axis, and since 2007, we've been creating resources to help connect parents, teens, and Jesus in a disconnected world. We're a group of gospel-minded researchers, speakers, and content creators, and we're excited to bring you the best of what we've learned about making meaningful connections with the teens in your life.

This parent's guide is designed to help start a conversation. Our goal is to give you enough knowledge that you're able to ask your teen informed questions about their world. For each guide, we spend weeks reading, researching, and interviewing parents and teens in order to distill everything you need to know about the topic at hand. We encourage you to read the whole thing and then to use the questions we include to get the conversation going with your teen—and then to follow the conversation wherever it leads.

As Douglas Stone, Bruce Patton, and Sheila Heen point out in their book *Difficult Conversations*, "Changes in attitudes and behavior rarely come about because of arguments, facts, and attempts to persuade. How often do *you* change your values and beliefs—or whom you love or what you want in life—based on something someone tells you? And how likely are you to do so when the person who is trying to change you doesn't seem fully aware of the reasons you see things differently in the first place?"[1] For whatever reason, when we believe that others are trying to understand *our* point of view, our defenses usually go down, and we're more willing to listen to *their* point of view. The rising generation is no exception.

So we encourage you to ask questions, to listen, and then to share your heart with your teen. As we often say at Axis, discipleship happens where conversation happens.

Sincerely,
Your friends at Axis

---

[1] Douglas Stone, Bruce Patton, and Sheila Heen, *Difficult Conversations: How to Discuss What Matters Most*, rev. ed. (New York: Penguin Books, 2010), 137.

WHEN THEY TALK, WE LISTEN.

SOCIAL MEDIA IS CHANGING day by day. What started as a way to connect with family and friends and share life has turned into marketing, advertising, and selling products to a larger online community. As many as 95 million photos and videos are posted to Instagram every day.[1] And 500 hours of video are uploaded to YouTube every single minute.[2] You can get lost down a rabbit trail of endless content that spans everything from funny dog videos to deep posts about religion and philosophy. That's a lot to keep up with—or compete with if you're trying to get your content out there.

If we were to be on social media platforms for only two hours a day, that would tally up to over five years of time over the course of our lives.[3] As of 2019, teens are spending more than seven hours a day using media.[4] That's more time than they spend sleeping at night sometimes. And with people in general spending more time than ever online, brands, movements, and celebrities alike have all realized the power of social media to persuade people to engage in a desired behavior.[5] As a result, a whole new animal has been born: *the influencer*.

WHAT'S AN INFLUENCER?

TECHNICALLY, WE'RE ALL INFLUENCERS in one way or another, but the term is used specifically to refer to a person who uses their social media presence and platforms to influence others to believe, buy, or do something (or commonly, all three). An influencer ultimately uses their power to market products (their own or someone else's) to their large online following, and by doing so, they also make money, which is why it's now considered a job.[6] Many influencers start out on Instagram or YouTube with a small audience and build it by posting consistently and making connections with their followers.[7] Typically, they make a name for themselves inside a niche and become an authority there.

You'll find influencers in every type of niche. They can build brands around anything—like eating healthy or creating art—and they share their lives with people who are eager to listen. Some examples are:

- Journalists who travel throughout the country and world, documenting their experiences

- Bloggers who write about everything from life experiences to product reviews

- Bookstagrammers who post photos of their bookshelves, current reads, and more[8]

- Makeup artists who post tutorials, share favorite brands, and more

- YouTubers who create daily content, including vlogs

- Video gamers who livestream video games and provide commentary as they go through different levels

An influencer ultimately uses their power to market products (their own or someone else's) to their large online following, and by doing so, they also make money, which is why it's now considered a job.

- Photographers who post photo shoots, projects, events, and more

In order to grow their platform and reach, influencers are on their social media platforms every day, engaging with their audience, growing relationships, and gaining trust. But for the most part, they don't just do it for fun; they want to monetize their accounts and get paid (e.g., by YouTube for views on their videos and/or by sponsors who pay them to market their products). And companies want to use influencers because they work. When an influencer you trust recommends a product, it feels the same as a friend saying they just discovered the best brand of mac 'n' cheese ever and you need to try it. It's a much more personal feeling than a commercial on TV, a billboard, a spread in a magazine, or a banner on a website.

WHAT'S THE DIFFERENCE BETWEEN A CELEBRITY AND AN INFLUENCER?

COMPANIES USE INFLUENCERS because they're *not* celebrities. People want to see what their peers are using and loving and give that a try. Unlike celebrities, influencers have built a network of people who know and trust them, people who see them as authority figures and are ready to listen to their advice.

There are differences between them (though these are slowly disappearing), and they typically have to do with how a person became famous. Celebrities are people who achieve stardom for something they do offline (acting, sports, politics, music, etc.), whereas influencers become famous for their online presence. If a celebrity doesn't ever create social media accounts (rare, but it happens), they are still known and have fans, but an influencer's fame *depends on*—and indeed is built by—their social media presence.

It's important to note that **Gen Z prefers influencers over traditional celebrities** because of their level of interaction and relatability. Celebrities are often seen as iconic, superior, unrelatable, and "other," whereas influencers are viewed as more accessible, relatable, approachable, and similar to their followers. As the Influencer Orchestration Network (ION) points out, "Social media influencers inhabit a place between celebrities and friends," meaning they feel like peers with whom Gen Zers have a relationship, but also like someone they can aspire to become.[9] According to a Google study, "70% of teenage YouTube subscribers say they relate to YouTube creators more than traditional celebrities,"[10] and ION says that

"Social media influencers inhabit a place between celebrities and friends," meaning they feel like peers with whom Gen Zers have a relationship, but also like someone they can aspire to become.

—INFLUENCER ORCHESTRATION NETWORK

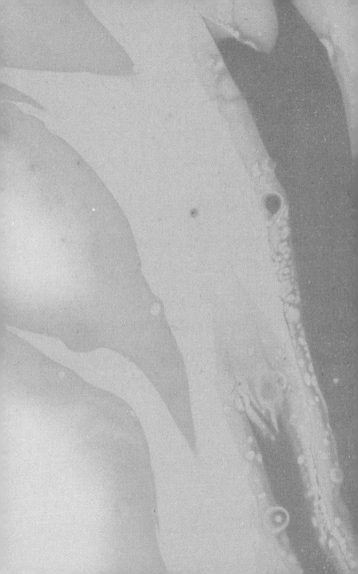

"social media creators get 12 times the number of comments that a traditional celebrity does."[11]

It's also important to note that celebrities and influencers are not mutually exclusive; influencers can become celebrities, and celebrities can become influencers—or it may be impossible to tell which one they were first (e.g., the Kardashians). In fact, nowadays people often become celebrities *only because* they already have a large online presence. Media companies tend to choose to hire the singers/actors/athletes who will bring fans with them over the ones who are virtually unknown. For this reason, many people feel the need to begin cultivating their "brand" or persona at younger and younger ages.

WHAT DOES THE BLUE CHECK MARK MEAN?

IT LETS PEOPLE KNOW YOU'RE LEGIT. Officially, it's called being "verified," and platforms use it to denote that you are who you say you are. They only do this for the accounts of celebrities, large brands, and influencers who have a large enough following (though the threshold for a check mark is not disclosed by the platforms). For more details on what the check mark means on different platforms—such as Instagram, Twitter, Snapchat, and TikTok—visit their websites.

WHERE DID INFLUENCERS COME FROM?

ADVERTISING AND MARKETING have changed significantly over the past few hundred years, with influencers slowly emerging thanks to the internet, social media, and the need for companies to find ways around ad-blocking software (which targets traditional online banner ads).[12] Combined with new abilities to harness word of mouth (which can lead to content "going viral"), marketers realized that younger generations trust product endorsements by people they feel as if they know (influencers) more than they trust them from people who feel separate and different (celebrities).

In addition, average everyday people realized that social media had effectively democratized fame, taking the power away from large corporations and media conglomerates and putting it in their hands. Anyone who wanted to get famous could do so simply by utilizing the power of social media. So more and more people started blogging, vlogging, making tutorial videos, putting their music online, and more in an attempt to gain followers and attract advertisers. For more on this, check out this fascinating article.[13]

WHY ARE COMPANIES WILLING TO GIVE THEM MONEY?

COMPANIES LOVE INFLUENCERS because they introduce products directly to the customers. An influencer may have fewer followers than a celebrity, but their audience is engaged and invested. One *Forbes* article explains that using influencers in marketing strategies costs a lot less than contracting big names (celebrities). And much like established public figures, influencers can introduce the product directly to a company's desired audience. But because it can be cheaper to use influencer marketing, companies can hire multiple influencers "for [a] fraction of the cost of a big name." [14]

When you see an ad pop up in the middle of a YouTube video, you might tune out or skip ahead, but influencers use their personal connections to make you want what they're selling. Instead of just putting a commercial in front of you, they weave products into their regular content. Because they're making real connections with people online, followers trust their recommendations. We trust the opinions of our friends, and companies trust the abilities of influencers to turn friends and followers into customers.

We trust the opinions of our friends, and companies trust the abilities of influencers to turn friends and followers into customers.

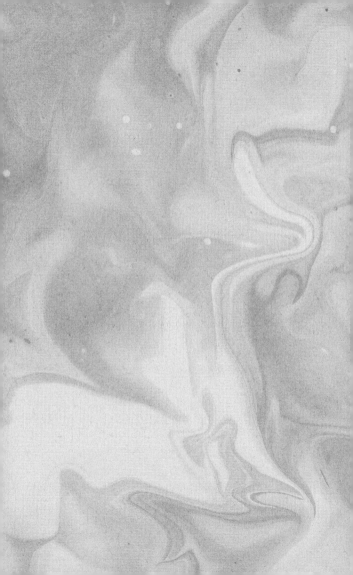

WHY DOES MY KID WANT TO BE ONE?

FROM THE OUTSIDE, being an influencer looks like a fun job. You become an authority on a topic you're passionate about and inspire others who want to follow in your footsteps. Influencers' feeds are aesthetic, their content is well thought out, and their posts can be insightful, fun, and humorous. One of the most attractive parts of being an influencer is the idea of getting paid to "live your best life" and do what you most want to be doing—traveling around the world like the Bucket List Family,[15] sharing fashion hacks like Hilary Rushford,[16] even playing video games like Ninja.[17] Pretty enticing, right? *Especially* to a teenager who already spends a ton of time on social media and thinks that "traditional" jobs are the worst thing ever. But, as we'll discuss below, being an influencer has its downsides, some of which might be worse than the drawbacks of other jobs.

One of the most attractive parts of being an influencer is the idea of getting paid to "live your best life."

IS BEING AN INFLUENCER AS FUN AND EASY AS IT SEEMS TO BE?

SINCE INFLUENCERS as we know them today wouldn't exist without social media, it follows that all the problems related to social media—obsession with image; comparison; preoccupation with likes, follows, and unfollows; number of views; time spent online; etc.—are there for influencers. But because everything they do is focused on social media, they may experience these problems on steroids. If your teenager wants to become an influencer, ask them to think about this: If they face pressure to curate a certain image or interact a certain amount or post often enough or look a certain way now, how much more so will those pressures increase if they try to make a livelihood off of social media?

One of the reasons fans often prefer content from an influencer instead of a traditional celebrity is because the layers of separation that exist between them and the celebrity are essentially stripped away with an influencer. There's no more mystery, no need for paparazzi to follow them around to find out even the tiniest detail of their personal lives. Instead, most influencers willingly share these details in an effort to become more relatable. Plus, followers tend to think that because they've faithfully followed someone and essentially helped propel them to fame, the influencer "owes" them things, like content every so often or personal glimpses of their lives.

One of two things typically happens to influencers. They either feel they can never turn the camera off and just relax and be themselves—they must always be on and ready to share their lives with the internet—or they become less and less authentic as they create a persona to share online in an attempt to keep some semblance of privacy. Neither of these is good, but they nonetheless happen because fans expect influencers to interact and be willing to show their lives, much more than they expect the same of celebrities.

These issues lead to another problem that's not obvious at first glance. What we see when an influencer posts an image or a video or other type of content is simply what they post. What we don't see is how long it takes them to create that content. So a teenager might think, *Great, a post plus a story or two on Instagram a day, a video on YouTube a day . . . easy! I can do that no problem.* But as some influencers are making more apparent (including YouTuber Jake Paul after vlogging for 500 consecutive days[18]), it takes a ton of time to make, say, a five-minute YouTube video or to get the perfect shot and write the perfect caption for an Instagram post. When your job becomes a 24-7 responsibility with no time off ever, that can lead to burnout and exhaustion very quickly. But it doesn't have to be that way. It's possible to set realistic expectations for followers early on by telling them when and how often to expect content, though posting less frequently typically leads to slower growth and monetization.

Beyond what we've already discussed, influencers also face pressure to conform to a certain image because their fans want it or because sponsors threaten to revoke their endorsements. There's also the fact that the internet can be a very cruel place. Anyone who is a public figure online is under constant scrutiny, with people waiting to pounce on anything that could potentially be controversial (one example is #CancelJames, a feud between YouTubers James Charles and Tati Westbrook[19]). Teens might feel pressure to pose in certain ways or in certain levels of undress ("Everyone else does it!"), or their newfound fame might open up access to drugs and alcohol. There's the possibility that your teen could be contacted by other famous people (as one teen was when she became famous virtually overnight[20]), and you wouldn't know about it or be able to stop it. "Managers" and "agents" who claim to want to represent your child may not have the best of intentions. None of this even begins to speak to the fact that teenagers are at a time when they're trying to figure out who they are, what they want, and what they stand for, so building a brand around something that could change a lot isn't always a good idea. The list goes on and on.

One of our staff at Axis remembers her mom always saying that she wouldn't wish fame on anyone. Though it didn't make sense to her teenage brain at the time, she now realizes that her mom was referring to all the pressure that came along with being famous. And it's only getting worse. If your teenager aspires to become an influencer, all of these things are worth discussing at length so they have a better idea of what they're getting themselves into.

Teenagers are at a time when they're trying to figure out who they are, what they want, and what they stand for, so building a brand around something that could change a lot isn't always a good idea.

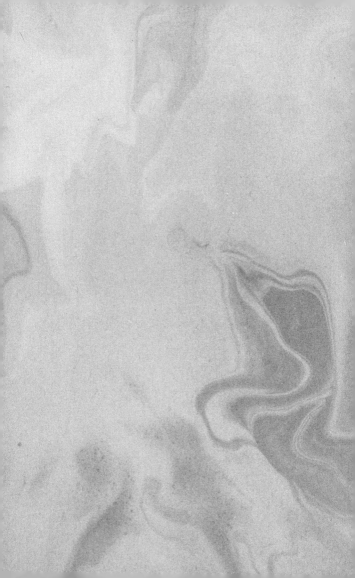

HOW DO I TALK TO MY TEEN ABOUT THIS WITHOUT SEEMING CONDEMNING OR IGNORANT?

WHETHER YOU'RE IN FAVOR of influencer marketing or not, you can and should converse with your kids about the *influencer* phenomenon in order to guide them toward wisdom and flourishing. Start by simply asking what influencers your teen has noticed on social media. Since teens are so involved on sites like Instagram and YouTube, a lot of their interests and ideas may be coming from influencers. By asking a nonthreatening question, you'll avoid putting them on the defensive. Take time to check out these influencers' profiles with your teen. This can help them to open up and share about who they're following. It can also give you insight into the world of influencers and the types of people your teen looks up to on social media.

Next, rather than just telling them what you think, it's important to ask questions that get them thinking. Some helpful questions include:

- What influencers do you follow? Why do you like to follow them?

- What makes this person qualified to give advice in this (or any) area?

- Do you know how they became an influencer? Does that make you trust them more or less?

- Is following them good for you?

- Is the influencer lifestyle really as great as it seems? How do you know?

- How can you be a positive influence on the people around you, whether that's online or in the real world?

- Is there a line you're not willing to cross in order to build your brand or make money? What is that line? How did you decide to put it there?

- How do you define success? What would it take for you to consider yourself successful?

- Is that different from how God defines success? If so, how?

- How could you use your "brand" as a way to reach God's version of success?

- If you became an influencer, how would you want to influence your followers?

- How would you use your influence to help others, glorify God, and bring true beauty to the world?

DOES SCRIPTURE SAY ANYTHING ABOUT THIS?

DOES IT SPEAK specifically about our modern iteration of what it means to "follow" someone or be an influencer? No, but as there's "nothing new under the sun,"[21] there's a lot we can learn from God's Word.

When we look at the stories told throughout Judges, 1 & 2 Samuel, and 1 & 2 Kings, we get a clear picture of how powerful influence can be. Before the time of the judges, Joshua had been a leader for the Israelites, one who devoted himself to following the Lord, obeying His commands, and not allowing himself to be influenced by the surrounding cultures. During his leadership, the Israelites also followed God, but after Joshua died, the Israelites slowly forgot about all that God had done for them (rescued them from Egypt, led them through the wilderness to the Promised Land, etc.), and they "did evil in the eyes of the LORD" (Judges 3:7).

Scripture tells us that God's anger burned against them, so He allowed their enemies to prevail. Eventually, they cried out to Him for deliverance, and He provided a judge to lead them in battle. For a time, they followed God again. But time and time again, they strayed, needed rescuing, cried out to God, were given a leader, returned to God, then strayed again.

As the Bible Project video on the book of Judges points out (see the link in the endnotes), the many judges who ruled over the Israelites during this time varied in their devotion to God.[22] And it's clear that the worse the ruler was, the more God's people strayed. Their influence made a tremendous difference. What's also worth noting is that, after a while, the Israelites got even more whiny, asking God why the other nations had kings and they didn't. God told Samuel that the

No one should have
more influence on what
we love, desire, pursue,
hope for, and believe
than God Himself.

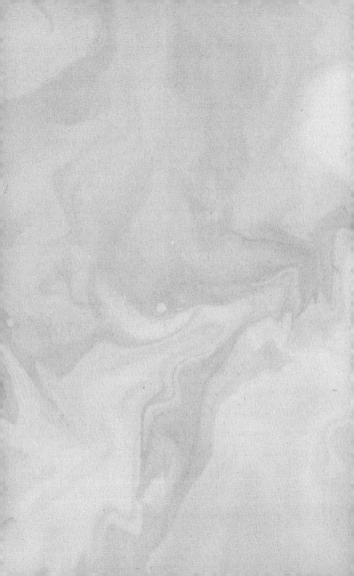

people were not rejecting Samuel by asking for a king—they were rejecting God as their ultimate King (1 Samuel 8:4-9). In God's good design, He was the Israelites' leader—their influencer—and they were His special people, set apart for His glory. Instead of embracing their identity, the Israelites looked at what everyone else had and wanted that instead. They were discontent because they thought others had it better.

There are *many* levels of influence, both good and bad, to analyze here, but what's quite clear is that no one should have more influence on what we love, desire, pursue, hope for, and believe than God Himself. If anyone else holds this power in our lives, we *will* be led astray. In addition, these Old Testament records illuminate just how much responsibility and power a leader or influencer has. It's no small task to be in such a position, and we are responsible for how we guide, teach, and influence others (James 3:1).

Other parts of Scripture worth examining with your teen include:

- Jesus guiding His disciples (Mark 9:35)

- Paul shepherding different communities of believers (1 Corinthians 10:23-29; Philippians 1:27-30)

- The serpent's influence over Adam and Eve (Genesis 3)

- Naomi's influence over Ruth (Ruth 1:16-17)

- Verses about keeping good company (Proverbs 13:20, Proverbs 27:17, and 1 Corinthians 15:33)

SHOULD WE ONLY FOLLOW CHRISTIAN INFLUENCERS?

HONESTLY, NO. Both Christian and non-Christian influencers can create great content, but the opposite is also true: both can create terrible content. Following influencers comes with positives and negatives, whether they're Christians or not. And just because an influencer calls themselves a Christian doesn't mean their content will actually be Christ-honoring or true. In fact, the Bible tells us to be wary of false teachers who disguise themselves (Matthew 7:15-20). Plus, within the Christian community there are so many different doctrines and beliefs that simply calling oneself a Christian doesn't tell us where someone stands on certain issues, let alone how they feel about promoting something simply to get a paycheck.

Ultimately, we should use discernment when deciding who to follow, no matter who they say they are. Outward appearances may be deceiving, and God tells us that He looks deeper than what we see on the surface (1 Samuel 16:7). In a world where people can so easily masquerade as anything they want, discernment is necessary.

In addition to this, we also need to be aware that even Christian influencers might promote things we don't need, because a brand is paying them to advertise. Not everything an influencer tells us to buy is something we need to have in our lives, nor should we value an influencer's opinion if it only increases our greed or dissatisfaction.

If we're unsure, we need to ask God to give us wisdom and discernment, as well as the strength to make the right choice. Sometimes we love things more than we love God, so even if they're not inherently bad, we allow them to take a place in our lives that is meant only for God . . . and we have to give them up. While this can be extremely hard to do, we need to ask God for His strength and determination to follow through—and we must teach our teens to do the same.

In a world where people can so easily masquerade as anything they want, discernment is necessary.

IF MY TEEN ONLY HAS A COUPLE THOUSAND FOLLOWERS (OR FEWER), THERE'S NO WAY THEY'VE BEEN CONTACTED BY SPONSORS, RIGHT?

ACTUALLY, IT'S POSSIBLE THEY HAVE BEEN. Brands love what they call "nanoinfluencers," or accounts that are pretty influential in a very small community and are willing to do sponsored posts for around $50 (typically younger teens).[23] Companies are starting to utilize these nanoinfluencers because they have the time on their hands to make creative posts that *don't* look like ads, they cost a fraction of most other ads, and they get pretty good results. So if your teen fits that bill, it's quite possible a brand has DMed (direct messaged) them asking if they'd like to "collaborate."

WHAT DO I DO IF PEOPLE START CONTACTING MY TEEN TO DO SPONSORED POSTS?

REGARDLESS OF WHETHER you decide it's smart for your teen to engage in this activity, *it's important to talk to them about it.* Anyone at any time can attempt to DM your child, even if their account is private. So if you never talk to them about it, they won't have your wisdom to guide them when it does happen. Ask your teen if they or their friends have ever been contacted by someone to do sponsored posts. What did they do? Do they wish they *could* do sponsored posts? Why or why not? Are they aware of the laws governing sponsored posts?[24] What would they do if someone wanted them to post something without disclosing that it was sponsored?

If, after lots of prayerful consideration, you do decide it makes sense for your teen and your family to do sponsored posts, it's important to set up boundaries and guidelines to protect your teenager. Make sure they know these guidelines, are willing to follow them, and understand that being an influencer is a privilege that can be revoked if they abuse it.

It's also important to vet brands and companies that contact your teen. Some are legitimate; others may not have good track records of actually paying or disclosing when their posts are sponsored. We encourage you to research the company reaching out to your teen and find out all the specifics included in doing a sponsored post before making a decision.

Some pros of doing sponsored posts are:

1. **The ability to make money in a field you're passionate about.** Not everyone gets a chance to do what

they love, and being able to make an income from sharing your life experiences with the world is a huge plus for a lot of people. You can also partner with brands you love, people you're excited to root for, and products that have changed your life.

2. **Exposure for brands and companies that are doing good in the world.** Some companies are working toward a better, cleaner, happier environment and are doing good by donating proceeds, among other things. Working alongside a company that provides clean water in other countries, for instance, can go a long way to enhance other people's lives.

Some cons are:

1. **Creating posts or an online persona simply for the sake of popularity.** It's a trap we can all fall into if we're not careful, and even doing a sponsored post can be inauthentic if the product is not something you actually support or use. One goal of sponsored posts and ads is to let your followers know that you're working with a brand. But if you're not clear about it, you can give off the wrong impression. That's why the Advertising Standards Authority (ASA) has come up with ways for paid content to be clearly marked, as described in this article.[25]

Not everyone gets a chance to do what they love, and being able to make an income from sharing your life experiences with the world is a huge plus for a lot of people.

2. **Overanalyzing every post and its reception from your followers by counting likes.** Teens spend hours a day on social media platforms, which include sites like Instagram and YouTube. With that much time scrolling through and posting content, teens can become pretty enamored with things happening in the online world.

3. **People who might try to take advantage.** Not only are certain brands and companies unethical, but as we mentioned previously, some unscrupulous people might try to offer their services as agents or managers for your teen. People like these are only there to prey on the vulnerable and take what they can for themselves.

CONCLUSION

INFLUENCE IS NOT A NEW CONCEPT. In fact, it's been around since the beginning of time. But it's never been so monetized or so tangible as it is in today's world. So even if your teenager never becomes famous or an influencer, there will always be people around them whom they can influence, for good or for evil. Whether they're online or in person, with a large audience or a small group of friends, you can encourage your teen to be a positive voice in their community and live a life of authenticity. While becoming an influencer is not inherently bad, it does come with a lot of risks and stressors, all things about which your teenager needs your guidance, wisdom, and, yes, sometimes even your protection.

Isn't that exactly what it means to be a parent? Yes, we're caretakers and providers and authorities and chauffeurs and cooks and cleaners and coaches and mentors and many other roles. But what it all boils down to is that we're the biggest influencers in our kids' lives. May we use our influence to point our kids toward flourishing, love, kindness, goodness, beauty, and, above all, Christ.

Whether they're online or in person, with a large audience or a small group of friends, you can encourage your teen to be a positive voice in their community and live a life of authenticity.

RECAP

- Being an influencer comes with both positives and negatives. It can be a great way to connect with people and a source of income for some, but it can also take up way more time and energy than "traditional" jobs—and it comes with unique pressures.

- Influence—both that which others have on us and that which we have on others—is not something to be taken lightly.

- God's Word is full of examples of influence used well and poorly.

- God Himself should be our ultimate influence. If something or someone's influence is more important to us than God's, then we have allowed it to become an idol.

- God can speak to us and teach us through both Christians and non-Christians, and both Christians and non-Christians can influence us for good or for ill.

- It's quite possible that your teens have already been (or will be) contacted by brands, thanks to the nanoinfluencer concept.

- Being an influencer is not inherently bad, but deciding whether or not this is good for your teen and your family will require lots of prayer, discussion, and wisdom.

- If your teen is an influencer or becomes one, make sure you set up healthy boundaries to protect them, and vet any and all companies who contact them for partnerships.

Influence—both that which others have on us and that which we have on others—is not something to be taken lightly.

ADDITIONAL
RESOURCES

1. "Rising Instagram Stars Are Posting Fake Sponsored Content," *Atlantic*, https://www.theatlantic.com /technology/archive/2018/12 /influencers-are-faking-brand -deals/578401/

2. "Understanding Influencer Marketing and Why It Is So Effective," *Forbes*, https://www.forbes.com/sites/theyec /2018/07/30/understanding-influencer -marketing-and-why-it-is-so-effective /?sh=395644f671a9

3. "Cameo, the Celebrity Shout-Out Startup, Nears $300M Valuation," *The Hustle*, https://thehustle.co/Cameo -startup-celebrity-shout-outs/

4. "The Increasing Allure of Being an Influencer in College," *Fashionista*, https://fashionista.com/2019/05 /college-influencers-brand -ambassadors

5. "For Brands of All Shapes and Sizes, Influencer Marketing Is a Serious Bet," *Quartz*, https://qz.com/1630285/how-brands-use-social-media-influencers-for-marketing/

6. Ray Vander Laan, *In the Dust of the Rabbi: Five Lessons on Learning to Live as Jesus Lived*, https://www.thattheworldmayknow.com/in-the-dust-of-the-rabbi

7. Check out axis.org for more resources, including *The Culture Translator*, a free weekly email that offers biblical insight on all things teen-related

NOTES

1. Werner Geyser, "What Is Influencer Marketing?—The Ultimate Guide for 2022," Influencer Marketing Hub, last updated March 2, 2022, https://influencermarketinghub.com /influencer-marketing/.

2. L. Ceci, "Hours of Video Uploaded to YouTube Every Minute as of February 2020," Statista, February 23, 2022, https://www.statista.com /statistics/259477/hours-of-video-uploaded -to-youtube-every-minute/.

3. Evan Asano, "How Much Time Do People Spend on Social Media? [Infographic]," Social Media Today, January 4, 2017, https://www .socialmediatoday.com/marketing/how -much-time-do-people-spend-social-media -infographic.

4. Kristen Rogers, "US Teens Use Screens More than Seven Hours a Day on Average—And That's Not Including School Work," CNN Health, October 29, 2019, https://www.cnn .com/2019/10/29/health/common-sense-kids -media-use-report-wellness/index.html.

5. Quentin Fottrell, "People Spend Most of
   Their Waking Hours Staring at Screens,"
   MarketWatch, August 4, 2018, https://www
   .marketwatch.com/story/people-are
   -spending-most-of-their-waking-hours
   -staring-at-screens-2018-08-01.

6. Dennis Kirwan, "Are Social Media Influencers
   Worth the Investment?" *Forbes*, August 21,
   2018, https://www.forbes.com/sites
   /forbesagencycouncil/2018/08/21/are
   -social-media-influencers-worth-the
   -investment/?sh=221f763af452.

7. Jayson DeMers, "The 7 Biggest Secrets of
   Social Media Influencers," Twitter Business,
   accessed March 8, 2022, https://business
   .twitter.com/en/blog/secrets-of-social-media
   -influencers.html.

8. Mara White, "#Bookstagram: How Readers
   Changed the Way We Use Instagram,"
   HuffPost, October 25, 2017, https://www
   .huffpost.com/entry/bookstagram-how
   -readers-changed-the-way-we-use
   -instagram_b_59f0aaa2e4b01ecaf1a3e867.

9. Eric Burgess, "Social Media Creators Are
   More Influential than Celebrities," Influencer

Orchestration Network, accessed March 8, 2022, https://www.ion.co/millennials-listen -social-media-creators-celebrities.

10. Celie O'Neil-Hart and Howard Blumenstein, "Why YouTube Stars Are More Influential than Traditional Celebrities," Think with Google, July 2016, https://www.thinkwithgoogle.com /marketing-strategies/video/youtube-stars -influence/.

11. Burgess, "Social Media Creators Are More Influential."

12. "Evolution of Influencers [Infographic]," No GRE, https://nogre.com/evolution-of -influencers/.

13. Danielle Hayes, "A Rousing History of Influencer Marketing (We Promise)," The Shelf, April 8, 2018, https://www.theshelf.com /the-blog/influencer-marketing-timeline.

14. Gil Eyal, "Fame as a Career Choice and the Rise of Micro-Influencers," *Forbes*, May 24, 2017, https://www.forbes.com/sites /forbesagencycouncil/2017/05/24/fame-as -a-career-choice-and-the-rise-of-micro -influencers/?sh=5d58e39f2cbd.

15. The Bucket List Family, Instagram, https://www.instagram.com/thebucketlistfamily/?hl=en.

16. Hilary Rushford, Instagram, https://www.instagram.com/hilaryrushford/?hl=en.

17. Ninja, Twitch, https://www.twitch.tv/ninja.

18. Geoff Weiss, "Jake Paul Breaks Daily Vlogging Streak to 'Help Some People That Are in a Lot of Need,'" Tubefilter, February 27, 2018, https://www.tubefilter.com/2018/02/27/jake-paul-takes-break-from-vlogging-to-help-people/.

19. Anna Quintana, "The James Charles Controversy Is Complicated—Here's a Quick Summary," Distractify, February 8, 2021, https://www.distractify.com/p/james-charles-controversy-summary.

20. Leah McLaren, "What Would You Do If Your Teenager Became an Overnight Instagram Sensation?" Guardian, July 22, 2018, https://www.theguardian.com/technology/2018/jul/22/what-would-you-do-if-your-teenager-became-an-overnight-instagram-sensation-.

21. Ecclesiastes 1:9.

22. BibleProject, "Overview: Judges," March 9, 2016, video, YouTube, 7:29, https://www.youtube.com/watch?app=desktop&v=kOYy8iCfIJ4.

23. Sapna Maheshwari, "Are You Ready for the Nanoinfluencers?" *New York Times*, November 11, 2018, https://www.nytimes.com/2018/11/11/business/media/nanoinfluencers-instagram-influencers.html.

24. Kristen Wiley, "3 Instagram Sponsored Post Laws You Need to Know," Statusphere, October 26, 2018, https://brands.joinstatus.com/instagram-sponsored-post-laws.

25. Amelia Tait, "Forcing Social-Media Influencers to Be Clear about #ads? Good Luck with That," *Guardian*, January 25, 2019, https://www.theguardian.com/commentisfree/2019/jan/25/social-media-influencers-clear-ads-celebrities-authorities.

PARENT'S GUIDES
BY AXIS

It's common to feel lost in your teen's world. These pocket-sized guides are packed with clear explanations of teen culture to equip you to have open conversations with your teen, one tough topic at a time. Look for more parent's guides coming soon!

BUNDLE THESE 5 BOOKS AND SAVE

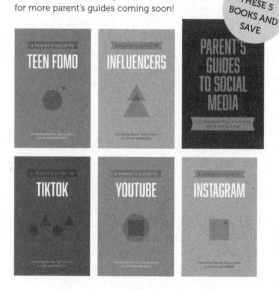

www.axis.org

CP1805